HOME POEMS

Antony Johae

For Isabel, best wishes,

Antony

ORPHEAN PRESS

2022

Antony Johae   December 2022

First published in 2022 by Orphean Press
10 Heath Close, Polstead Heath, Colchester CO6 5BE

Typeset in 8½- on 11-point Typotheque William Text,
printed and bound in Great Britain by Peter Newble:
10 Heath Close, Polstead Heath, Colchester CO6 5BE
peter@newble.com ÷ www.newble.com

ISBN 978-1-908198-24-2

British Library Cataloguing in Publication Data
A catalogue record for this book is
available from the British Library.

For my grandchildren,
James and Adora

CONTENTS

ACKNOWLEDGMENTS

MY thanks are due to members of the Colchester 'Mosaic' Stanza of the Poetry Society, and to members of the Suffolk Poetry Society, for critiquing some of the poems; to Peter Ualrig Kennedy of Poetrywivenhoe for editorial advice and to Peter Newble at Orphean Press.

Thanks also to the editors of the following publications where versions of the poems in this collection have previously appeared: *Carillon*; *Decanto*; *Dempsey and Windle Newsletter*; *Dial 174*; *Earth Love* magazine; *Earth Love: An anthology of environmental poetry* (Earth Love Press); *Essex Belongs to Us: Writing about the Real Essex* (Amazon); *Est: Collected Reports from East Anglia* (Dunlin Press), *Freedom Poems: A Poetrywivenhoe Tenth Anniversary Collection* (Dunlin Press); *The High Window*; *The Journal*; *London Grip New Poetry*; *Long Poem Magazine*; *Militant Thistles*; *The New Verse News*; *On a Knife Edge* (Suffolk Poetry Society); *Orbis* Quarterly International Literary Journal; *ornith-ology: the poetry of birds* (Poetrywivenhoe/ Mosaic Stanza); *Poetic Scents along the Talbot Trail* (Sudbury Café Poets); *Poetry and Audience: Poetrywivenhoe Anti-Covid-19 New Poems Initiative*; *Twelve Rivers*, magazine of the Suffolk Poetry Society; *Without Walls*, a poetry anthology of new works in aid of Colchester's homeless (Musket Books).

INTRODUCTION

IN the early 1950s, my mother returned to Colchester, in north-east Essex, to set up her business. The town then became my home base as well. Her family, the Rowleys, had moved from London to Mersea Island in the 1920s. They also resided for some years in Colchester where my mother attended the Girls' High School. It is fitting, therefore, that *Home Poems* should first focus on both the island and the town.

My connection with Suffolk goes back to 1945 when I was sent to a boarding school in Felixstowe; I passed six Spartan years there. Much later, in more comfortable retirement, I became a member of the Suffolk Poetry Society. The four poems in the third section derive from this more recent association.

Because both my mother's and my father's families were London-ers, the metropolis has never seemed far away. Indeed, I spent a number of years in my youth and early adulthood living with my grandparents (those on my father's side of the family) who had re-mained in the capital. And even after moving back to Essex, I found visits to the big city were an essential source of mental stimulation. The poems in this part of the book look back briefly at my early days in London and then move forward to the experience of more recent times. Also included are poems of 'other places', some set near to the capital, while others occur as far away as Australia.

The fifth section, entitled *Offspring*, is devoted to my two child-ren — sometimes in nightmarish fashion, and to their offspring — my grandchildren to whom this collection is dedicated.

The penultimate section, *Eco Poems*, begins in neutral vein with aesthetic images drawn from nature, but, as the theme develops, the language takes on a didactic tone appropriate to concerns about the way we treat our planet.

The poems in the final segment, *Creative, Critical, Philosophical*, range from the rigours of poetic formation and its attendant rewards, through to the strains of relationships, the fortunes of politics, the power of protest, confrontation with illness, and elegaic offerings of praise.

Contemplation of metaphysical presences brings the collection to a thoughtful close.

THE AUTHOR

ANTONY Johae was born in 1937 in Chiswick, Middlesex, and educated at St Felix School, Felixstowe, Suffolk, and at Bradfield College in Berkshire. He trained as a mature student at St Osyth College of Education, Clacton-on-Sea, taught for a year at a primary school in Hackney, London, and went on to study English and European Literature at the University of Essex, post-graduating with a Ph.D. in Comparative Literature in 1979. He has taught at the University of Essex and in Germany, Ghana, Tunisia and Kuwait, during which time he has published academic articles in international journals.

Antony retired from teaching in 2009 and now divides his time between Colchester and Lebanon, his wife's country of origin. He has previously published three collections: *Poems of the East* (Gipping Press, 2015), *After-Images: Homage to Éric Rohmer* (Poetry Salzburg, 2019) and *Ex-Changes* (The High Window, 2020). *Lines on Lebanon* is a work in progress.

I

MERSEA / BLACKWATER

SAILING INTO SILENCE

for Rod Usher

We are out on the Blackwater
my uncle, my cousin, my brother and I
with motor chugging, sails unfurled.
We've set off on a rising spring tide, choppy
with the wind from the west breezy
to leeward in the bright midday.
Uncle spits out orders — mains'l's hauled up
flapping in the slack; jib's full
yearning seaward beyond the estuary.
The engine phuts off ... silence ... silence ... quiet as Quaker calm ...
deep, deep ... time's held fast, avast, avast ... nature's opened ...
hush and gentle swish through water
sail filled, rattle of boom let out, we heel,
pull ropes tight against the wind, cleat them
and tack off towards the Bradwell Point.

Now my uncle's tranquil at the helm
with wings drawn on fair and friendly thoughts
his worthless worries left on Mersea's shore;
and standing tall at the prow, cousin Chris
whose best boat, and hope, got storm-smashed
one night, thrown up on Brightlingsea wall.
Timothy and I sit small in the cockpit
in thrall of high water, unsteady heaving sea,
wind's keen gusts, the lurch and shudder
as we go about — gybe — and rush fair wind away from land.

Our father loved his ocean-goer, *Mina Dhu*;
he'd tie up in North Sea ports,
anchor off cosy Jersey coves,
pass lit liners in the night, dark cargo ships,
wave back at passengers on Channel ferries,
mark trawlers' trailing nets, look out for bobbing buoys
and with lovely land in sight follow courteous pilots in.
In war he took Dunkirk soldiers off
then laid her up and waited for the end,
for he found peace in thinking of the moment
sail would unfurl, chugging stop, and immanent silence enter.

FROM ISLAND TO BAY

for my cousin, Mehalah, in Australia

You were a girl of seven or so
bred on east coast saltings,
your home, *The Victor*, nestled in sea mud,
your purview Mersea's sundry folk[1]
when I saw you last on moving stairs at Baker Street[2]
before your *Fairsea* passage to the far antipodes.

Removed, you said, from hemisphere to hemisphere
— estuary's black water to the shark blue of the Bay;
transplanted, you said, from the Island's heavy clay
to François Peron's red peninsula.

But you being Baring-Gould's girl[3]
kept the Strood, the Ray, and The Rose in view[4]
— would remove them to Denham[5]
where you potted cross-legged girls
or painted sea-grass swirling,
these to be marvelled at by travellers in your quayside studio.

Now you bring full cups to the Cloud's two tables
where Denham's denizens come to read in the Bay's breeze
or gather for conversation as convivial as Fountain, Victory, and Lion,
haunts of the Mussetts, Wyatts and de Witts
who with raised glasses drank to the men as the smacks came in.

But alack!
You found the Bay's hot winds, red earth's dust, and unpeopled places
belied the Island's creeks, its channels and North Sea chills,
its characters, contours and yesterdays,
and could not match pleasant Mersea memory
with the all-too-plain present of Shark Bay.

---

[1] Mersea Island in the county of Essex

[2] Baker Street in London

[3] Sabine Baring-Gould, author of the novel *Mehalah: A Story of the Salt Marshes* (1880)

[4] The Strood — causeway between Mersea and mainland;
the Ray — island between Mersea and mainland;
The Rose — pub at Peldon

II

COLCHESTER / CAMULODUNUM

FLYING CAMELS

My road is Roman;
it straddles the old wall
down to the Quaker burial ground.

Where the cedar grows
it bends towards the park
heading west to the foot of Balkerne Hill.

I pass where a gate once was
triumphal perhaps with legions passing
recalled now on moss-covered plaque.

Caught in a cold easterly
I mount the steps to William's castle
to the shelter of its tall walls.

My walk-thoughts wander south
to winter sun, hot behind car glass,
to desert seeds grown to yellow flowers.

I reach the place where children play
and see beyond on mansion's well-kept lawn
three camels, tethered, courtesy of Ryanair.

Colchester
20 October 2009

FLYING AWAY
IN FALL
for Thérèse in Lebanon

Seeing leaves come down
and flocks in flight cross the sky
I long to wing south.

Colchester
21 October 2009

8

ON MY WALK

I saw them in Castle Gardens,
dog chasing a cat as though it were a hare,
cat run like a fox hunted by hounds;
she jumped to mount a fence, fell back,
did not know the pursuer found it fun,
hissed at him and scratched.
The dog bit back; cat screeched,
then away she ran.

I saw a swan from the Colne river bank
trying to cross a weed-green weir,
her cob waiting in the tidal water below.
The pen found a footing, heaved up her weight,
poised for a moment on the threshold
and fell, wings flapping, to the hard ledge beneath.
I thought she was hurt, but when I returned at dusk
she had swum away with her mate.

PLUCKED
for my brother, Tim

After springs absent from England
these daffodils planted on verges and embankments
by boroughs determined on colour
strike home from traveller's coach window.

They ring early bells, lean like expectant crowds,
sun-yellow in the Essex easterly.

One thinks of William wandering with Dorothy,
daffodils dancing in lakeside breeze to nature's ways,
pensive poet's recall in creative solitude.

We drove, my brother and I, along Remembrance Avenue
one day this spring, saw dear daffodils
flat, lying by the roadside
plucked.

INVITATION TO DANCE
for Tim

You took every chance to dance, like a firebrand,
with all and sundry at the Club
in those early days at the Albert pub
with Tom Collins and his trad jazz band.

You advanced, like a lion, at Abberton,
engaged local girls, pert and pretty,
and weary weekenders down from the city
in a jaunty jive not to be forgotten;

took novices in hand at the House between the Stockwell Streets,
swung them into swinging sways
and turns to make them giddy and amazed,
enough for tender feet to dream of dancing in their sleep.

At the Rovers Football Club in Stanway
you approached women thick and feline,
small and tall, spirited and benign,
strutted and stomped with them in remarkable display.

On the move to Marks Tey, you danced with yet more agility,
combined jitterbug with deft salsa steps,
skipped with your partner in a polka and — lest anyone forget —
switched from one to t'other in adept versatility.

Loyal to the last, your faithful Club attendance,
the filling of an empty floor with Muriel's swirling magic,
Lynn's delirious jive, Maureen's strong stomp, Diane's tread to music
— all this coined by you in *The Spirit of Jazz*, in the spirit of your dance.

ST MARTIN'S-BY-MY-MOTHER

In Quaker Alley, between the Stockwells, stands St Martin's,
empty of church trappings save the Lord's table and rood.
Its composition: slim bricks and flint rubble, bare means
at one with the saint's origins and deeds;
he who in a vision at Amiens' gate, with soldier's sword,
on impulse cut his cloak in two, giving half to a hapless beggar
bare in the winter cold.
This story told, Martin became beggars' saint;
of wool weavers and tailors too.

In Tours, loath to become bishop,
he took to a barn, hid among geese, their gaggling giving him away.
Thus sat he with mitre and crozier, disheveled and distraught,
in apron-shaped amice, chaste tunic, and girdle.
His feast falls in Fall when geese gather to migrate.
Martin is their saint. Rich in fare, the bird's consumed
at lantern procession in Catholic lands particular.
Vintners and innkeepers also revere him
glad of late-grape harvest.

But there's no chalice in this church
though vault is barrel,
floor unsteady.
There's no wall ornament,
windows are plain;
no pews,
few seats
nor any vestment.
St Martin's unclothed, like the beggar at Amiens' gate.

COMMEMORATION DAY
AT MYLAND CHURCH

Inside the church we hear of men at the Somme
suffering, trench-sloughed, ready to clamber up and over
into earth-squelch, barbed-wire-hindered;
Fusilier Packer framing his final words in a sodden book
knowing he will not come back;
Corporal Lane — a letter to his love — sickened by want and war;
Private Delmuth hoping he'll be hit in the imminent slaughter
— not dragged back minus limb or loins;
and Lieutenant Cleeve, of the artillery, ready to fire,
whose girl writes to him from a munitions factory.
On the other side, Medical Officer, Stefan Westmann,
tent-bound, bandage-ready, morphine-prepared
for men shattered by English shells.
The congregation is asked to sing 'The King of Love'.

Outside the bugle blows, flags dipped in deference to memorial-named,
. . . cold silence . . .
bugle blows, dismissal. The dark crowd drifts, departs.
I see someone linger, last to leave — young and bent,
open coat flapping
jabbering tongued confusion
trousers hanging on
drivel-mouthed
fathom-deep face,
head colour-crowned
in fool's hat — green-blue-yellow-orange-indigo-violet-red.
In this light I ask myself who it is insane.

Written on 18 November 2016, marking the hundredth
anniversary of the end of the Battle of the Somme.

13

UNIVERSITY
OF ESSEX PIE

This is a week of student pies,
savoury and sweet — topping free.
You'll notch up plenty of points:
we've moved a decimal two points to the right,
so don't forget to bring your phone
for topping up.

An octogenarian responds:
I am on the point of impatience.
I thought you said topping was free
yet you want me to tap an app;
it seems to be beside the point
— so much pie in the sky.

TREE GREETINGS

It irked at first, this Essex message:
'Season's Greetings from the Alumni Office.
See the holiday tree in Square 3.'
I asked:
Why 'holiday'?
Why be shy of Christ's Mass?
Is this tree unworthy?
Is the Lord's name hidden in shame?
Or do I detect secular correctness?

These queasy questions vexed like gnats in the night
coming back time and again to suck
away at the day's good cheer
and resolutions of the imminent year.

Then a mind-window opening they flew away,
Light pouring in on HOLY DAY.

III

FELIXSTOWE / SUDBURY

FROM LANDGUARD POINT, FELIXSTOWE

Late November, and day lies low
over the estuary; the sun finds its way through
white cloud, dazzling the sea with sheen.
On the far shore, Harwich is caught in lustre,
church spire rising in aspiration towards the light.

Over the Stour, the sky darkens in storm,
is blown towards us in a rush, ruffles
the mirror, breaks it into pieces
as squall—whistling—hits dock cranes,
rain sheeting down against the metal of my van.

I picture the fishing fleets once afloat in tempest
out in the German Sea after herring haul,
sails unfurled, caught with their catch;
and today's weighted freighters impervious to wave
ploughing calmly through the globe's oceans.

SCALE

Cycling through the Suffolk countryside
I thought:
How small the winding lanes
rose-strewn cottages
patches of yellow wheat
half-hidden streams
hummocky hills.
How small they all are!
Then at the hostel
two boys from Jersey
said with homesick sighs:
'Here everything seems
twenty times as big.'

THE GREAT BLONDIN

In 1859, you tight-roped your way across Niagara Falls
trundling a wheelbarrow, bag of potatoes full.
Again, covered in a sack from knees to head,
down the rope slope and up to cliff edge.
You took the Manager on your back —
a man your weight — made light of such freight;
sat down midway, cooked an omelette — and ate it;
stood on a chair in the air, one wooden leg settled on the rope.
You coped with crossings in blindfold, and somersaults on stilts
in Paris, and between the transept of Paxton's Palace;
amazed spectators in Edinburgh's Gardens,
in Dublin's Portobello quarter,
and on Birmingham's reservoir water.

In 1872, when your fame had reached great heights,
you deigned to come to Sudbury Town
to trip, without tripping, the wire fantastic.
Its citizens came in scores to see you elevated and acrobatic,
you who'd walked on wire in Liverpool Street,
a London kid strapped tightly aft — yet another high-spirited feat.
In Sudbury, behind Friars Street, they stared agape and aghast
to see you push a resident held in high regard
across the open Anchor yard in a one-wheel barrow.
Escape was never narrow for you, a high-flying *artiste*,
nor for the brave heart game to be carted.
They called you The Great Blondin, who nineteen times, never stalling,
tight-roped Niagara's Falls — and made it without falling.

Based on sculptures depicting Sudbury's heritage, this poem and the
one that follows were performed at the Suffolk Poetry Festival in 2017
(Sudbury Café Poets). They have appeared in *Poetic Scents along the
Talbot Trail* (Sudbury Tourist Information).

WILL KEMP'S JIG

I am he who plays with Master Shakespeare and the Lord Chamberlain's Men,
William Kemp, known for making mad jests and merry jigs on theatre boards,
The 'dunce' who bet he'd dance to Norwich from London town
In ten days — or less — for a hundred pound.
Would you want to read about it there's *Kemp's Nine daies wonder*
For purchase at Nicholas Ling's shop in the city by Saint Paule's.

This tale tells how on first Lent Monday, I with my 'tickle it good' Taberer,
Bee my servant, and Sprat appointed overseer, set out for Essex County
Frolicking to foot it in my buskins, a doubtful crowd following,
They opining I would give over within a mile of Mile-end.
They did not know my heart's like cork, my heels feathers,
That I could fly from here to Rome with a mortar on my head.
So lightly I tript forward with much a doo through Ilford, Romford, Burnt-wood
For Chelmsford, and onward to Braintree morricing in mud.

On the fifth day, in Sudbury, there came a burly fellow of the South Folk,
A butcher boasting he would jig with me to Bury. But hardly had he measured
    half a mile
He stopt his morrice, breathless, and complained:
'You'll not see me keep on, even for a hundred pound.'
— With that he lay lax in a field on the ground.
There happened a lusty country lass, brown as a berry, among them treading in
    my steps.
'Boy! You're a faint-hearted lout!' she called out loud.
'See if I can't hold out for one mile!' — at which the crowd laughed heartily.
'Nay,' she protested. 'If the Dancer will lend me a leash of his bells,
I will venture to tread one mile with him meself.'
Seeing her tuck up her russet petticoat with mirth in her eyes and boldness in
    her words,
I garished her well-larded legs with said bells and with a smooth brow
Bad Tom Taberer strike it up. Then to our jig and jumps, the maid and me, we
    fell.
She danced in the piteous heat with a wild will did this well-made maid,
Her hips a-going a-swig a-swag, her brown brows a-sweating varnish.
When I purchased her a skinful of drink at the inn, and put an English crown in
    her palm,
Modestly she dropped me some dozen of short curtsies, and I, giving her thanks,
Took back my bells and, like Old Hamlet, bid her 'adieu, adieu, remember me'.
Thus morriced the maid with me to Melford, it being a long mile.

To cut a long tale short, I, Will Kemp, morriced merrily from London to
   Norwich City
In less than good time, my fame among the North Folk having gone before me.
Now you'll see my beaten buskins, them I danced in from London thither,
In memory nailed, twofold, to the Guild Hall wall.
'He be as tough as old boots,' I heard a citizen say. 'It were a far-gone feat;
Pity his pains to jig in nine days near on ninety mile.'
'My Gin-ess me,' quoth one wit. 'It's enough to go in a book of records.'

IV

LONDON / AND OTHER PLACES

BAR ITALIA

1949–present

1957

I used to go there, to Soho
from Piccadilly for a quick lunch,
or after work, with colleagues from the office,
to take a slow cappuccino.

This was London's Italian time:
Fellini at the Classic, *Roman Holiday* at the flicks;
Milanese styles — slick in West End windows —
and at the Bar Italia, Marino Marini singing on 45s.

There I tasted my first pasta — *alla Napoli* and *Bolognese*,
took in southern ambiance, family familiar,
waitresses warm in their service,
barmen bantering in another tongue.

I was young and green in those rock and roll days
before affairs and unrest took me away.

2022

Now it's Bowie and the Bee Gees, but not at this bar
where the jukebox gives out a crooning tune,
the women still serve their family fare
and parleying barmen pull at dripping dispenser.

Rocky Marciano is still the boxing hero,
never knocked out, never lost, the poster tells us;
black-and-white photos of people from the past,
famous then, kept alive on bar wall.

The floor's customer-worn, the same tall stools,
colour-faded Formica to rest a cup,
sugar canister, generous as before.
I face a large glass — it reflects the past.

On the counter, an old cash register — it pings,
pasticcini on several shelves below,
not factory cooked but candid,
antidote to corporate cake and coffee.

Better to bend it, Juventus play Roma
on wide-curved screen, changes to be expected,
as are pavement tables and chairs for smokers
and inside, stiff drinks for worn-out workers.

In sum, Bar Italia remains a family concern.
Long may it last until I next return.

27

ON CANARY WHARF

Tall blocks hide the sun, throwing shadow on long walkways;
they funnel a fall wind, chilling my brother, his beloved and I.
We see Lehman's people exiting swing doors,
revolved into the cold of disuse.
They'll take the light train, the last, to encumbered homes,
their wonder descending into worry.
Some take unusual time outside, are collared by reporters,
speak of bewildered accounts into camera lenses,
are quizzed into repetition of a morning only part unfolded.
Coppers stand by fretful of demonstration
in the stark square; they help lingerers move on
like mourners gravely after burial.
We wander the cool dock, unpeopled by the draught,
she clinging to Tim's tight arm, I zipped up;
on moving stairs descend to shops and stalls and stands,
bright boutiques and warm cafés. We drink hot chocolate,
cream-topped, watch short-cropped city-suited men pass,
some passing time, and girls in office frocks conversing.
All this while all that is solid melts into air.

Monday 15 September 2008

28

IN WESTMINSTER SQUARE

From Crystal Palace I took a '3'
through the town's encumbered boroughs
past Lollard's Tower, over Lambeth Bridge
to mock-gothic palace and the land of sovereign ministries.

From the top I saw them ranged by a manly statue,
Star of David waving blue and white in the wind
and a banner bearing telling words:
'We will never stand alone.'

I thought of refugees withheld in Arab camps
left alone, waiting to go home;
should have got off and questioned them,
these men and women chanting for their nation,

listened in a Quaker way, friendly and attentive,
but sat still on the upper deck mentally unmanned
as the bus headed up Whitehall to high hero
guarded on four corners by his fighting lions.

Aboard the '3' next day, I had in mind to act,
found the statue unmanned
and across the road, flag-free peace tents placed in long vigil
on the square's hard foundation.

CONFERENCE

You came from Africa and Asia, from Europe too,
met on a morning in Bloomsbury Square,
shared lines lyrical and stories magical,
our minds, cosmopolitan, gathered for a day
before, much said, you went away.

STREETWISE

It is starting to rain.
Umbrellas are going up, but I don't own one.
In Oxford Street they're going home,
but I don't have one.
I take cover in a station entrance.
The air smells wet, car tyres hiss,
and I shiver.

I settle by the river.
It is night and I lie under the sky's roof.
I stare at the stars and at the moon's fullness
and wonder if there are better places.
The pavement penetrates my bed
of newspapers and squashed boxes,
and I shiver.

There's a girl not far off in a corner.
She talks to me and I get up.
She's running from a father who beats her.
She's cold and says she's hungry.
I go to buy her a burger with my last pound.
When I get back I find her in my sleeping bag.
She takes the burger and tears at it. A wind bites,
and I shiver.

We lie in the bag together.
She sleeps — I feel her warmth
and catch the heat of her breath.
I sleep too and dream of another planet.
I wake at first light and find her gone.
There's a note: 'Thanks — see you again.'
It's going to be a warm day.

ON THE TUBE

I face five passengers.
Four finger their phones, send messages
or play games in fixed stare.
The fifth reads a book — *Vanity Fair*.

SENIOR OFFERS

I am on the tube
hanging on to a grip,
in thought.
I see myself in the glass.
I look quite young — and feel it too.
A freckle-faced woman beckons.
'Would you like my seat?'
I decline. Doors slide open
and I get off
minding the gap.

I am at the airport
hanging on to my bags,
in haste.
I see myself in the lift.
I look so fit — and feel it too.
A chic check-in woman beckons.
'Would you like a wheelchair?'
I decline. My bags disappear.
I feel insecure
passing through Security.

JOURNEYING

AT GATWICK

09.05 touch down . . . long taxi to the gate . . . engines whine off
— click of seat belts — rush to take baggage down;
some wrap up against expectant cold,
others finger cell phones before the door is opened.
I sit at the window and look down on bleak-black tarmac . . .
We descend unwieldy steps uncertainly — walk laden to the gate,
up a flight, breathless, to a cold corridor. Behind the glass
I see chains of seats but no passengers departing . . .
a woman flips quickly through my marked passport pages . . .
I haul off my present-packed case from the belt,
exit the green door, look for signs to the station.
'No train today, sir, take the coach' . . .
I hear an urgent shout: 'London, Victoria!'
My case wheels into me — unbalanced — I fall
knee-first wrist twisted, lie on my back amazed.

IN THE COACH

I pull back my trouser leg to look at my left knee;
it is scraped red, tender and stinging; move my wrist
(my writing hand) aching from the fall. The coach is full,
air close, leg-room small. I let drop my trouser leg;
the cloth settles on the wound. I feel like a trencher
transported from the front, headed for a camp hospital.
From the window I see the mass of south London suburbs passing —
neat, between-wars semis, parks of leafless trees, industrial terraces,
shabby high-street shops closed for repose, a red-brick supermarket
with car park empty, hospital — I feel my knee throbbing, wince,
and imagine my wife's surprise when she sees me on the step . . .

AT VICTORIA

Taxis line the rail-station rear where the coach has pulled in.
I ease myself down the steps, clutching the rail — feel an ache,
struggle to gather my luggage with my left hand . . .
It's a long hobble to the underground; the street is empty of traffic;
I hear the clack clack of my wheels on the Palace Road pavement;
. . . at the Circle Line entrance there's a grille across the opening.
I look around me; the main line station gates are barred,
turn towards the forecourt and see no red double-deckers,
but taxis with 'For Hire' signs lit up waiting in silent rank.
A lost couple ask for a road in Bayswater (where I once lived);
my gammy hand points northward and they give thanks. . .
I make for the coach station, the one that serves the nation,
but not this morning — not to any destination.
I have a yawning sensation as though it were the world's end . . .

I tap on '£200' and the notes come out . . .
'How much to Colchester?' I ask a wrapped-up man in his cab.
He gets out his papers, shuffles them around.
'Three 'undred quid, mate' . . .
Now I am looking for a box to phone home — a sort of SOS —
from a man stranded with a stinging knee who needs to pee,
an easterly cutting him down like the *Deutschland* in December.[1]
Shop doors are closed, lights out; here a café with its shutter down,
news-stand with no papers, glass doors to offices unguarded,
nor any porters watching over Belgravia's posh apartments;
and in this apocalyptic street — Mac's fast food shut up.
Back down the Palace Road I hear a flapping,
look up and see flags flying from a tall Edwardian building
— colourful crosses, stripes, stars, a sun, partial moon,
and one in white with name imprinted in spindly letters:

THE GROSVENOR

I look around me in relief. The cloakroom is marble-clad;
a yellow light warms it; taps are golden, the porcelain riddled with age.
I pull up my trouser leg — I have never seen such searing red —
and knee-dab gently, painfully, at the graze with the water running.
There's nobody about, no attendant even to tick me off or take my tip,
so I'm not embarrassed to be leg up in this palatial place,
only anxious that someone will pass through the polished door — and catch me . . .
The cubicle is cosy with its wood finish, the phone shiny clean,
purr on the line clear; my pound drops down and I dial . . . *drrrr-drrrr*,
drrrr-drrrr — familiar English sound — then on the line
a voice more than familiar, my daughter — I am instantly transported . . .
Tables are laid with white cloth, cutlery and crockery crested,
twosome cruets set side by side. A cup of coffee keeps me company
in this vacant place, the waiter waiting as I watch the heavy clock . . .
I am sitting at a window — my cup empty — on the look-out for the driver.
There's a view onto the street, onto the grey pavement
but I see no people, just a pigeon hunched up on the wind-swept ledge.
Through the glass I remember . . .

FENSTERBILD

. . . I remember our strolling here, in this street, oblivious of buses,
coaches, cars, taxis, vans, lorries passing, before we parted,
you for far Germany and I for the Faraday Exchange;[2]
heedless, too, of the pavement crowd hurrying from work to the station.
You were lovely in the late afternoon, your dress girlishly flared,
your face flecked with freckles — *Sommersproßen* smiling back at the sun.
Our fingers touched as we walked; my right hand took hold of your left.
We glanced at one another shyly in the first ache of love, words tumbling
hilariously from our lips, your laughter drawing me out, wit keen,
not as when in Haymarket coffee bar we heard the Berlin Wall go up

and you distressed, I in my raw youth could not share the hurt.
Nor when a Caribbean man, lately settled in her Majesty's realm,
charmed you in Queensway and I contracted green-eyed pain.
But now, our fingers intertwined, forbad mourning, albeit you were leaving
on the cross-channel train. My father and your friend to whom you wrote
(her name's forgotten) stood with us on the platform startled into smiles
by our affection. The whistle blew, we lip-kissed lightly, doors slammed,
jolt forward . . . I saw you wave out into the open, your dark hair flying,
and when the last carriage had gone, pictured your mother at the *Bahnhof*
waiting — and you, in winter, on your way to school
— I felt a throb of loss . . .

ON THE ROAD

. . . feel my knee, skinless, stuck to my trouser leg,
see the Thames in a calm emptiness from the window,
Embankment queerly quiet, no Tower queue,
street market gone from Stepney, no bells at Bow.
This high-walled motorway I've not seen before
cutting through London's east to Stratford flats
and on to Gants Hill's repeated streets,
to familiar Romford roundabout,
thence northeast to open Essex road.
Dead elms line the sky, fields fallow and sown fly by,
red-roofed farms, weather-boarded barns, lone bungalows
and gross overspill estates — all this glanced at
as the driver, talking of his many journeys without stop,
transports me in ghostly time to England's ancient town.
This is an avenue of remembrance tree-lined for the dead
and there's an elephantine water tower atop the built-up hill.
Here's High Street strangely draped in red and green
and William's Castle silhouetted in the late light.
We swing into Roman Road,
the driver stops his talking,
drops me cursorily in the cold . . .
a tree in the window flickers fitfully,
I take in the quiet,
stand on the house step stiff-wristed with my case,
feel a leg-twinge,
press on the welcome bell
and (so to say) fall on my knees with thanks.

25 December 2007

---

[1] The *Deutschland*, caught in a northeasterly gale, went down in the Thames estuary in the early morning of 7 December 1876. See Gerard Manley Hopkins's poem, 'The Wreck of the Deutschland' (1918).
[2] The Continental Telephone Exchange at Faraday House in the City of London.

LOCK KEEPER
AT LALEHAM
(near Heathrow)

Shirt tight against his breast
sporting shorts dangling from his waist
head shaven and shiny
he could be some television wrestler
as he elbows muscle-brown punctured arms
on open gate.

At seven he retires to the keeper's house
leaving late boats to pass through unaided.
They'll rope a bollard
cleat to make fast
scramble ashore
turn an easy wheel
see sluice-swell
gates drag through the water.

A holiday boat chugs out; they see me in sailor blue
wearing what might be a captain's cap
leaning on the rail, old and water-wise.
They raise their hands in shy parting
and I mine with an approving smile.
It is as if in times past
I had turned the spoked wheel to flood the basin
and with my weight, heaved open the heavy gates,
I, the lock's ancient keeper.

NATURE AT LALEHAM

'Tamesia House' lies by the Thames,
so too 'Merry View' and 'River Holme'
watchtower rising through its roof.
There's 'Tiny House' and double-garaged 'Barn'
and 'Halycion Court' where dwindling days are spent.
'Four Seasons', 'Belmont' and 'New Timbers' line the path
their hedges cut back, willows weeping, trees trimmed,
garden, newly-laid, with CCTV curbing shrub thieves.

The river's rich suburban too:
Silver Lass, slender white, knotted to landing marked 'PRIVATE';
canopied *Cecilia*, streamlined *Circassia*, double-decker *Marlan Deux*,
little *Alouette*, swift *River Hawk* and new *740 Super Cruiser*
all moored along the stretch where I stroll.
Blue Tail Fly's a tender made in glass fibre
but *Thelma*, ancient umpire launch, is left to rot.
An old canal barge passes, holiday-maker at the helm: *Nice Butt* . . .

The towpath proffers canoodling wooden seats
tucked away in bushes by the water
one in memory of long-standing servant of the realm.
I am walking this safe way back from the lock
to Laleham's fenced tents and motor-homes,
hear the whine of rising aircraft,
look down. Stop. See it slither across my path
slim snake unhurried curling towards the tangled bank
see it slip silently into the stream.

ON CLOSING THE
CAMMELL LAIRD
SHIPYARD, BIRKENHEAD

1938,
the year of *Kristallnacht*,
sees a worker walking the cobbles
in the awful morning. A gas lamp
lights the thoroughfare still,
a hoarding exhibits its patented product,
an uncoupled cart bends on the curb;
terraces loom into an unclear day
and repetitive roofs mount the street
stacks sticking into the industrial air:
all this, living for the yard.

There are no cars in this quarter of Hands
nor antennae colouring the world.
Only angled black cranes — though redundant now —
tell me of that time:
they rise scraper-like over the town
athwart the great slim silver ship
floating almost in the sky
ready to slide on completion into the ocean
a bottle to be broken over her bow
her name to be written on her prow:
Ark Royal. Man of War.

DOWN UNDER

We came, my daughter and I, in a fresh year
through the heavens and the clouds
to land on the Continent's scorched-red soil.
Before me lay the city's bright sights;
but I did not look up at the Southern Cross.

I did not look up
but was struck by sales, singers, and street flesh,
I, worried by price and provision;
and when Earth cast its shadow on the moon
I did not look up at the Southern Cross.

MY COUSIN MEHALAH'S RAY

With the dogs you walk along Denham's shore[1]
daily. They romp and splash and dash
after the chucked ball,
bring it back, wait on the watch
for your next delightful throw.

Out over the ocean the Sun's burning,
the wind's coming in cooling;
you sit on the sand, port in hand,
gazing at white-horses.

Earth turns, day declines,
fire, water, meet, merge
ember red on the horizon;
curve seems to sink,
to be slowly sea-consumed.

Just once you saw the green ray[2]
flash out over the coral bay.
You could happily have wished that day
to be transported to Mehalah's Ray.[3]

---

[1] Denham, Shark Bay, Western Australia

[2] In Jules Verne's novel, *The Green Ray*, the lovers discover one another at a moment before the sun disappears below the horizon and when a green ray becomes visible for a few seconds. Éric Rohmer takes up this motif in his film, *Le rayon vert*. See my poem, 'Delphine' in *After-Images: Homage to Éric Rohmer* (Poetry Salzburg, 2019).

[3] Ray Island lies between Mersea Island, on the Essex coast, and the mainland. Mehalah is the eponymous name of Sabine Baring-Gould's heroine in his novel, *Mehalah: A Story of the Salt Marshes* (1880).

V

OFFSPRING

ANNA

Deep she lies
in cloth to her chin
lids in sleep
skin heat-spotted
curly-headed red
like baked earth
or sweet Mother
with faint brows
to pencil in time.

She turns away
my brother's ears
to eye me with smiles
not the lying ones
I have lain with
but familiar copies
as snaps or glass
expose who got us:
Father.

Now unwrapped she sleeps
limbs out
as petals in the deep day
white on the water
rest before frogs
and lips are pink innocent
telling me to stay.
I begin
a prayer for my daughter.

DEATH OF MY DAUGHTER

A nightmare

I saw my father's house
like a crofter's cottage
stone-made in a grey terrain
the slate roof with its original slant
a wall shielding it from sea storms.

I saw my daughter laughing on a sofa
floating uncertainly on rough water
and an old smack
with sails full in the wind
most beautifully riding the waves.

I should have boarded the boat
to bring my daughter to safety
but impulsive love told me to sit by her;
the sofa overturned
and threw the child in.

I looked with a dreadful intensity
at the grey mass
but could not make her out —
heard only the raging waves
and the piping of her laughter
as she went down.

TO MY GRANDSON

I come to you,
to the far Antipodes,
my child's child
to hear you named in WA,[1]
James Antony, willed
by Anna and by Will,
testament to their keen desire.

The last name's one to last along the line
like trees whose branches spread through time;
the middle is mine.
The first's uniquely yours
given in mutual grace by William
with Anna to first son, James,
on this high November day of names.

---

[1] Western Australia

MY DAUGHTER
CHRISTINA'S DESSERT

She gathered blackberries in country hedgerows
put them on a silver dish
brought them home to wash
ready for the table.
She placed meringues on each bowl's base
encircled them with late and luscious strawberries
tipped thick cream moat-like around
sprinkled sugar sparingly
took up her wild berries
and placed them dark against the sweetened whiteness.

Her offering up
we sat down to a lasting supper.

IRRESPONSIBILITY
A nightmare

I told my daughter to go and play
yet I knew the terrain was dangerous:
the gorge soared up to a cleft cliff
while the World revolved away from the Sun.
But I could think only of the wood,
of cypress and cedars and forest flowers
and branches and bunches to take home.
I did not think of her with the mountain goat
nor of the despotic bird who carries off the lamb.
I forgot the fearful chasm and the night
falling fast after the green ray
had signalled Earth's departure.

Then a dreadful dawn broke in on me.
I picked up the sticks
to put them under my arm
but could have flailed myself with them
for my failure.
Then I let the sticks drop
for I could see only my daughter
lost on a ledge
moving blindly towards the edge
in her piping innocence.
My cry came out dead and mute.

IRONING MAN

Adora, my daughter's daughter,
born 20-9-20
has rained on me ironing aplenty,
not to mention other garments
put in the basket by her parents.
It's now three weeks on
and I don't know where the time has gone
getting crease and damp out of one-piece baby suits,
cotton covers, flannels, towels and cute
little bonnets and hats. They come in a pile
after a final spin; are hung up for a while
until ready for my job at the board
— no sooner finished than there's more from Adora's hoard
to hang up and dry,
to flatten, sweating, with heat on high
making them fit for baby to lie on.
If I'm going to keep up, I'll need to be a man of iron.

KEEPING IN TOUCH
WITH MY
GRANDDAUGHTER

The more I think of Adora the more I adore her.
But Cancer and Corona have parted us,
she gone to a Levantine labyrinth,
I remaining solitary in a straight kingdom
to be by my ailing brother — bedridden.

But WhatsApp has aptly rendered her present,
her baby image visible,
quickening squeals audible,
spell-like smile — so lovable,
etched over the ether on an old man's heart.

On the screen, I see you stare back.
I coo to you and you beam,
chit-chat and your hand reaches out,
you thinking I can be grasped
like you do sweet mother.

If I cannot be clasped as you would
your father's strong arm
or nestle in grandmother's pillow-breast
I can be there for you virtually
and be touched.

VI

ECO POEMS

TULIPS
IN A VASE

You are no still life
framed on a white wall.
Your stems do not pose;
splayed, they bend and lean.
Some seem to yearn
— look at yellow-petalled,
how she stretches
strongly upwards
like swan's wings;
and subtle purple sink
as though suffering,
while another rises
in ascension;
droop of two-toned
goblet, first to expire
in vase's white water:
tulip time curtailed.
You are no still life.

DANDELIONS
IN A VASE

You are no unwanted weed.
I picked you
between nettle and grass,
saved you for my green vase.
You stand there, stems poised
in upward curve,
ray-floret flower
open to window light.
When the sun's low
petals contract into sleep,
breath held in water.

END OF AN OLD OAK

Snow lies on bare branches.
They have come to cut you down.
A bulldozer scoops up earth
— thrusts at you.
The men fix harness to a trembling tractor.
They chop, hack, heave, saw.
Hot motor drones.
Harness is jerked tight.
You shudder and snow falls.

The men breathe out hot air,
rest with hands on hips,
resume hack and heave.
Motor drones on,
rope tugged.
I hear a groan, rumble,
see at first a slow topple, tumble,
quick crash into broken branches.

The men stand back and gape at
wide-girth trunk,
branches snow-scattered.
I feel guilt for them
these executioners of civic orders,
men whose lives depend on it.
They'll rest easy with their wives tonight
and come back tomorrow to burn you.

POET'S GALLERY OF WADERS

for John Hall, M.B.E.

VANELLUS VANELLUS
In black and white the Lapwing flocks
wheeling through winter skies,
in spring scatter to mate, males tumbling
with piercing 'peewit' cries.
Nested on simple scrapes in mud or sand
she sits with plumage iridescent green with purple sheen.

Predators are mobbed when nest's at risk
distracted from eggs and foraging chicks.
Lapwing's on red list:
if ceasing their wheeling in winter
and tumbling in spring
their 'peewit' call will be one more missed.

PHILAROPUS LOBATUS
Red-necked Phalarope is pot-bellied, short-legged, needle-billed.
She is more beautiful than he;
it is she who competes for breeding ground and site to nest,
she who seeks out her male to mate.
He is incubator, his sober colour camouflage.
She guards him against females that trespass
and when chicks are hatched, leaves the male to mother them.

RECURVIROSTRA AVOSETTEA
Scarce wader, Avocet's
long black upturned bill sweeps
from side-to-side in shallows.

GALLINULA CHLOROPUS
Moorhen's ubiquitous, almost a landlubber, even climbs trees,
is laboured in flight;
seeks out succulent snails, fish, insects, and stray berries.

Moorhen male swims to mate with bill in water;
they nibble at one another's feathers,
will defend twig-built nest to the death.

FULICA ATRA
Relative to moorhen,
Coot's more attached to water,
will dive for invertebrates,
eat waterweed
squabble over surfaced catch,
not like ducks who fare with neck under.

ACTITIS HYPOLEUCUS
Green-legged sandpiper
teeters when standing in wading waters;
is stiff-winged in flight.

NUMENIUS ARQUATA
'Cur-lee, cur-lee' is their call.
They stand tall.
Body's mottled grey and brown;
pink under, bill curves down
peg-like. Legs are bluish, rump is white
in a wedge when wader takes to flight.
'Cur-lee, cur-lee' is their sound,
Curlew their proper noun.

CALIDRIS CANUTUS
These journey from Arctic in winter to temperate lands
hardly stopping on long migration
to muddy estuaries, finding rest on high tide roosts.

Knots know echo-location:
sentient bills probe sand, saltings, and mud,
detect invertebrates, molluscs, and crustaceans,
a cull close to eco-location.

PLUVIALIS APRICARIA
In summer, Golden Plover is not all golden
but black-throated, band of white on belly and chest,
black back, cap gold-spotted.

In winter, chest and belly turn yellow
approaching precious name.
They gather together on black waters.

PLUVIALIS SQUATAROLA
Like some reiterated dance of death
Grey Plover stands, watches, and waits;
when ready, runs forward,
pecks kiss-like at prey;
stands again, watches and waits
and when ready, runs forward
pecks kiss-like at prey . . .

TRINGA OCHROPUS
Elegant while eating on lake edges, marshes, pits and rivers
Green Sandpiper sinks to sewage works for sustenance.
As it stands on green legs it bobs.
Disturbed — dark green body zigzags into the air.

TRINGA NEBULARIA
Here's another with green legs; elegant too,
chases invertebrates and fish, keen-eyed
in shallow water. Grey bill lightly upturned,
it too is of the sandpiper breed
— named Greenshank.

TRINGA TOTANUS
This bird poses on post
rests on fence
reposes on rock:
red-legged Redshank.

CHARADRIUS DUBIUS
Little Ringed Plover's
black eyes are ringed in yellow,
circle of infinitude.

CHARADRIUS HIATICULA
Ringed Plover has no ring
but is rotund.
Its taps to sand and shingle
tempt invertebrates to the top,
they mistaking foot-trembling
for raindrops.

Feet apart, off the ground,
this wader has white wingbar
and is widespread.

HAEMATOPUS OSTRALEGUS

After summer breeding on inland fresh water
these 'peepers' winter by the sea
with birds come from northern places.

Shellfish are to Oyster Catcher's taste:
mussels are hammered, cockles prised open
in a feast of *fruits de mer*.

In the air they're winged black and white,
beak, red, pointing the way like fighters
on a striking sortie.

PHILOMACHUS PUGNAX

Not Pope or Ruff of fish stock,
    long-necked, small-headed Ruff are fawn-brown, pale-bellied.
But breeding males trump others;
    they sport bright-coloured ruff, feathers raised around the neck
like Holbein's high citizens; and tuft to head as tassel to cap
    of old nobleman's bright son.

CALIDRIS ALPINA

Dunlin is not dun, nor dusty;
in the fair season, brick-red above,
black patch to belly.

CALIDRIS ALBA

Much travelled Arctic breeder, in winter common to British coasts,
little Sanderling feeds in small flocks from long sandy strand.
No water-walking or mud-probing for them
but scampers back and forth, like children challenging incoming waves
at tide's edge, only these antics are for insects, worms, crab, stray fish
— and stinging medusa.

GALLINAGO GALLINAGO

Snipe nests in scrapes,
swallows crustaceans whole,
bisects insects with long bill;
drums when courting,
tail feathers vibrating
in darting downward swoop.

ARENARIA INTERPRES

Turnstones do exactly that —
creep on rocks, flutter, flip them over on their backs.
They find food there: birds' eggs, chips, and snacks;
bigger still — maybe mouse or rotting rats.

NUMENIUS PHAEOPUS

Seven-whistled Whimbrel's a lovely sight in flight:
down-curved beak thrust forward as though supersonic,
blue-grey legs tucked away as undercarriage,
white wedge and streak on tail and fuselage,
wings agape in flocked formation.

RALLUS AQUATICUS

Water Rail sounds like a piglet squealing,
but to say it lives in a sty would not be appealing;
reedbed is actually where it's sleeping,
is a secret, so please stop peeping!

SCOLOPAX RUSTICOLA

Short-legged, dumpy Woodcock's last to be versified;
not too hard to recognise
it being brown
with darkling bars across the crown;
hides in dense cover
and unlike Plover
sharp tacks when disturbed,
sign that she's perturbed,
then drops down
to the ground
to undergrowth hideaway.

Like many wetland waders
Woodcock's numbers are dangerously down.
Wetland abused is habitat reduced.
If we don't wake up, their numbers will be up.

Adapted from the Essex Wildlife Trust Website, www.essexwt.org.uk

OIL
Dover—Ostend

That great long black creature
floating on the water
is not a whale
deposed king of the ocean.
It is a tanker.

THE PIGEON

I saw a pigeon pecking itself.
It had oil on its white front.
Each time it pecked
it looked at me
with a glassy eye
as if to say:
'Man, that's your fault.'
Then with a limp
it hobbled off
leaving me
with my conscience.

HENS' LIVES
for Ann Keelan

PROLOGUE: LITTLE HENS RESCUE
Sylvia received her dispersed chickens
consigned from hen-hell for re-homing
eight scruffy ones among doomed thousands
released from battery-bondage.
But these hens, being egg-bound, wasted after maximum lay,
sickened and singly dropped dead to Sylvia's dismay.
Little Hens Rescue like hens' hospice.

1. ANN'S HENS
Not so Ann's hens: they range happily garden-free
in health and longevity — five favoured fowl
fond consumers of corn, crisps, chips and all that's take away,
tinned beans, blackberries, cashew nuts and cheese,
raisins and ripe lettuce before reaching the table.
In line and bottoms up by garden fence
they rummage under shrubs at times particular
or below Camellia for hapless hurrying ants.
These are creatures of routine who after school bell
parade on house drive before passing pupils
perchance for adoration.

2. HAZEL
She's wise, outwitted fox,
still survives, feeds from Ann's hand,
perches on her knee, or rests slowly stretching languid wings;
legs and feet follow by degrees,
toes curling and uncurling in the garden heat.
In rain, head feathers stick up punk-like — and on her ginger neck.
Hazel's not vain:
on daisy days you'll see her face absurdly petal-covered
like paint at a children's birthday party.
Be warned though — this bird's tranquillity disguises no humility:
if Ann and Rich, forgetful, fail to pen hen-house by dark
she'll stop at Richard's window, peck petulantly at his glass
remindful of his obligation to afford her
her rightful place at the peak of the pecking order.
Nor is she lazy, lays without fault
streaked eggs ending in overlay, cock-like in rococo swirl,
and daily delivers a whopping pearl.
Work done, settled by snug boiler in blissful snooze
she'll not dream of factory, battery or broiler
but take comfort in the Keelans' appetizing garden.

3. AMBER

Amber's angel white
silk-soft and downy, but oddly drawn to dirt.
In the wet her feet are crusts of mud,
flesh-crest black, nostrils dirt-rimmed.
Stain-drenched as tea poured from pot
her feathers stick flat to a pitiful frame.
Next day, angel-hen's miraculously white again!
In summer when Ann settles down to sandwiches
Amber joins her on garden bench in expectation of
crunchy crisps and cheese bits — a luscious *dejeuner à deux*.
But she's more an indoor creature when door's ajar.
Standing on kitchen floor, she'll oversee her mistress cooking;
when fridge is opened look to check what's there;
and larder — on the lookout for raisin store;
meal over, stare mesmerized by dishwasher's chug and hum
and when motor's off, sneak past Rich for kip in Ann's armchair.
Amber is most sociable; she perches hawk-like on Richard's wrist,
barrels up to Ann across the garden, first to be picked up, petted
and on cold damp days nestles her fond wet head in ample bosom.
She talks too — with a coo when Ann once ailed — and daily
with dual-pitched squeak joins in by way of piercing conversation.
Because she's favoured hen and owner of such acumen
Amber doesn't doubt she's human,
thus egg-lay is contract-limited to every other day,
small, glass-smooth; but when yellow's tasted
turn out intense as hen's ecstasy.

4. HARRIET

Harriet is French-speckled — *Coucou Maran* —
proof against rain, as smart as Coco Chanel,
never looks bedraggled; takes to sulking under
Ann's parked car at first show of shower.
She seems at once malignant — pink-eyed evil — but that's a lie
for she's fond-friendly.
Oft will she squat hunch-shouldered,
puss-like, for balmy back-rub
or clasp clean pink toes to proffered finger
and with closed eyes purr when foot is fondled.
But there's fair exchange when mistress takes doorstep tea;
she'll settle on Ann's left foot dispensing hen-heat to her.
As for pecker: spoon-fed beans' the thing,
even better — remains of *Chow mein* imbibed from silver carton
leaving Harriet's mouth a saucy orange.
As for eggs, the writer has no data to date,
whether they're large or small, brown or white, plain or ornate.

5. NERA

This is the prettiest of hens:
calls up pictures of Dégas' fashioned widow,
wholly laced, quietly be-jewelled.
As per her name, Nera's painted black as night;
she's brilliant too — shines green and blue in certain light.
Needles golden as fairy tale mark her ebony breast
and arrows strike gold under precious chin
like Chinese pheasant in antique objet d'art.
But Nera's flighty — perhaps because she's pretty.
Coming for customary back-rub,
when human hand's held out,
she'll nimble-footed leap from reach
as if to snub the hand's possessor.
Or is she inclined to tease, one wonders,
or simply hard to please?
Although seemingly superior
it's not seen as infra dig by this bird
to wallow without reserve in dust-bath hollow
close by fresh plant, Ann's favoured flower,
or on Richard's new-laid lawn.
But eggs too are new-laid — Nera's are deep dark brown —
not to be beaten.

6. TERRY

Theresa-May is pterodactylic, her feet crocodile-navy, hyper-huge,
outer toenail black, middle varnished opal-white.
Such large footwear confines her to a gangling gait as ungainly as
dangling line.
This one's no beauty: pigeon-turkey looking, her coat's a gloomy grey
except when caught in evening light and feathers strike out blue.
Not sociable, she'll retire behind Rhododendron glumly
while the others promenade ensemble around the garden gaily.
Nor will she be picked up whatever temptation lies on hand
causing Ann to wonder how this hen's blue cotton-wool behind
stays unsullied when she'll have none of patron's chicken grooming.
Terry's tough, wins squabbles over apple cores and too-ripe peaches,
plucks unsuspecting butterflies from the sky, and when done
will take a sip at water dish insensible to disjointed bits
protruding from imbibing beak — wing one side, leg t'other.
To her credit Terry's eggs are long and slim, bullet-shaped and weighty
— not to mention tasty.
But you'll not find them in the usual hen-house place
because she's sorely idiosyncratic as befits a bird that's pterodactylic.
To collect Terry's heavy eggs you need to be strong and tall
for, you see, she lays them on the garden wall!

These are Ann and Rich's prized family of five
who thrive like the lords of poet's 'Penshurst'
in hen's first ethos, natural cosmos,
enjoy benefit of abundant garden
and with well-laid plan deliver new-laid eggs
rounded as the season's cycles,
as tasty as Ann's sweet trifles.
This is no half-way house from factory hell
nor hospice where death-knell will shortly toll
but a homely haven in Dartmoor Devon
where you'll find Ann-made Little Hens' Heaven.

RED LIST

Perdix cinerea is partridge, mottled brown, freckled front, sides barred chestnut.
Of the *Colombidae* clan, turtle dove, noted for constancy, makes earthy love-calls.
Finch-like corn bunting, coded *Emberiza calandra*, chit-chits and chuckles.
Of the genus *Motacilla*, slender-billed yellow wagtail, another fêted farmland bird
Listed.

Wood warbler, lemon-yellow at the throat, from *Sylviidae*, trills at growing tempo.
On stiff wings, lark-like tree pipit — *Motacillidae* — parachutes when it sings.
Willow tit of *Paradae* progeny, repeats triple zees, perchance *ipse, ipse*.
Woodpecker — lesser spotted — *Dryobates minor*, plumage black, red, white,
and humble bunnock among the country's woodland birds
Listed.

Even *Turdus merula*, once common blackbird, last songster of the day
and *Turdus musicus*, fine-tuned throstle, speckle breasted
Listed.

If these were gone from Britain's shores, so too their airs, ambient hues,
numinous names — and what's more, they'd fade from every poet's word-store.

WIPING THEM OUT

We're told that it's a 'new formula' and 'a major step forward',
that we should welcome the world's greatest producer
of insecticides.

They've doubled the killing power and put it in a bigger can.
You should shake it like a cocktail to mix
the poisons,

point the nozzle at the beast, press the button down
and squirt it — *pif* once and he'll run, *pif* twice and he'll
drop dead.

We're told that there'll be no more bugs in our bathrooms
or cockroaches in our kitchens if we purchase
this pesticide.

You call it 'Green' even, when it slaughters as $(CH_2Cl\cdot CH_2)_2S$
did the men in trenches, though these creatures wear no masks
to stop the gas.

You call it 'Green' when each squirt, pushed out under pressure
sends vapours upwards to O_3 — buffer to ultraviolet —
and depletes it?

Better let the roaches roam a little in the spare room.
If not, they'll stay while we, cocksure of the future,
will wipe ourselves out.

FALL

Nearly November —
mosquito, butterfly, rose
— climate is changing.

VII

CREATIVE,
CRITICAL,
PHILOSOPHICAL

WRITERS' BLOCK

For Jacques Derrida, Gayatri Chakravorty Spivak,
Jean-Jacques Rousseau, James Joyce and Franz Kafka

That dangerous supplement of an artful pen
worlding of words; of maps made
from the mind or memory
or inventions wrought in dreamed-up places
lending Earth its contours,
its isthmuses, straits and gulfs.
More even: its philosophies and politics:
capitals, frontiers and dominions;
satellites, republics and imperial provinces.

That dangerous supplement, mute word
naming the unnamed; the beast its species,
the thing its class, text type,
fabrication or fabulation on silent white,
form-gotten moments. The future's
contained, plotted, timely, provident.
When done, the go(o)dly writer cutting a nail
turns to lust through a window
sickened by the marriage bed.

That dangerous supplement, Jean-Jacques' death
where speech is obliterated denying presence,
cheats discordant nature of its voice and song.
The young culprit of motion, health and consanguine pride
dreams only of desire, desires dream
of giddy height and sight of then and now and when,
a blended sign of singular value
as angels traverse dichotomous day or momently
blade or rope or bullet touch the man condemned.

CHOOSING BOXES

In my dream, two boxes hang in the air.
I know one to be pepperoni,
the other four cheeses.
— I picked them from the freezer yesterday.
Now they're suspended
like marionettes without strings,
and I can't tell one from the other.
How to choose from these choice boxes?
Then, like a poet dredging deep down,
choice words float up — I wake up.
They seem like a resolution.
I rise from my bed and write them down:
The less egg the better.

FLYING

Flying boy, the way he twirls in the air
or on his bike takes off over hill hump.
How the water-ski girl, hair horizontal in the wind,
glides across the bay like a sea-plane;
surfers poised on white waves
who come in on curving crest upright for the shore;
or those that run fearless over cliff's edge
and hang like crowns in the currents of the air.

Take a trumpeter hitting a high note,
how he makes it stretch towards the sky.
O that I could fly so with verse!
Not like Hamlet's words, words, words,
but keen and quick and winged and terse.

WILL'S TESTAMENT

They say Sir Walter came back smoking from Virginia,
That his cleaner, thinking him aflame, put him out.
Now they're saying Will Shakespeare smoked too.[1]
They've got some pipes he might have drawn on
For inspiration at the Globe, or sweet verses to his Earl,
Stratford pipes — bowls and stems — tested
To see what Will imbibed
Beyond nicotine, camphor, or *Cassia aldehyde*.[2]
Were there hallucinogens in his trunk at Abingdon?[3]
Erythroxylon or 'noted weed'?[4]
Not posh garment or bane of garden
But Assassins' grass smoked knowingly
With quill in free hand dressing words afresh?
I say, what matter if Will did not will them.
He has willed his verse to us.[5]

---

[1] See the article 'Much Ado about Coke — signifying Not Much' by Ann Donnelly, Museums Curator of the Shakespeare Trust, in which she refutes suggestions that Shakespeare may have smoked hallucinogens.

[2] Donnelly: '"Cassia Aldehyde" [is] derived from plants of the genus "Cassia", including C. "fistula" from India (also known as "pipe tree").'

[3] The article states that traces of cocaine (*Erythroxylon*) were detected in a pipe found at Abingdon in Oxfordshire. Whether Shakespeare smoked a pipe there, or even visited the place, is another matter.

[4] The Director of the Shakespeare Trust notes that in Sonnet 76, 'weed' refers to clothes used as a metaphor to denote use of language.

[5] See Sonnet 135 where Shakespeare puns on his first name.

LOVE'S LABOURS

The girls dance as they have been taught
pas de chat, grand jeté, arabesque and *relevé*.
They repeat and repeat
arabesque, relevé, pas de chat and *grand jeté*.

Beautiful as these are, their language carries limitation.
The dancer's arms stretched out lack wings,
long legs leap but land.

So too a poet's repertoire of words
confined to sign, sound and knowing tropes
to craft and artifice
— habitual toil and iteration.

But the dancer's diligence sees the psyche soar,
the poet's graft gives rise to soul.
In the dancing and creating
Love's labours are not lost.

TWO HAIKUS

Could Antigonus,
wasted by babe and bear, land
on Bohemian sand?

Kafka on the shore
of a sea-less land stands un-
sure on strand's quick sands.

LOST
DOSTOEVSKY

It was on the library shelf;
the spine announced its title
— *An Honest Thief* —
cover red, letters yellow.
Now it's not there.
I look for loaners,
search library stacks
as if for a lost pin
— or stolen?
but not by any honest thief.

COLLOCATIVE
CONUNDRUM

With my yellow pencil
I draw a rainy tail
upon a bushy hill
frothing with fierce flowers.

I tell a steep story
about an exciting lion
basking in sharp water
dallying in the deep day.

GAMES

The boys are playing in the park;
one dribbles and shoots;
he doesn't score — the coach keeps goal.
They tackle and run past two girls watching
eager to kick the ball; but when it comes at them
one winces and crosses her arms.

At school I was one of those afraid of getting hurt,
couldn't kick a ball, but still gave words a shot,
tackled and ran with them,
a score aimed without flaw,
or so I thought given extra time.
When a poem's done, it's a word game won.

SHE IS A POET!

She is a poet.
Manipulation is not needed.
Words rise up from inside.
The first stage flows fast in a narrow stream,
the second broadens into slow thought — branches into imagination;
the third sees a mingling of fresh idea with the salt of past practice.
See how her poem comes into being!

Why then has she put down her pen
shut her laptop lid
picked up hammer and nail
to mend a broken house?
Its windows are many,
frames, paint flaking,
shutter hinges loose.
Such work will close off word-spring.

PC PAIN

You spend your time on Windows,
don't send me messages.
I feel the door to you is bolted.

OFFERINGS ON
VALENTINE'S DAY

He gave her a red rose.
It pricked and drew blood.
She gave him a cake — heart-shaped
in a box — past expiry date.

MADONNA AND BOOK

It comes from pilgrimage, this statuette
set on the top shelf by her bed,
right hand on heart, left half-open,
fair face a quiet smile.
She's clothed in a white gown to her feet —
the folds can be felt — and up to fragile neck.
White hair, parted, is young
glimpsed under veil reaching to hidden waist.
This Mary's magnific, alabaster pure,
without spot, white hot with Love.

On a shelf below, by her bed,
three dark volumes, *Fifty Shades of Grey*,
whip, rope, blindfold, chain,
amatory cold, novel attachment, torture, pain.

SONNET À BOÎTE

This place is low with light
in moving colour — red, aggressive,
smoke-fused, amber, orange. Bright
spots fasten on close dancers, suggestive

of hot blood, rehearsal for the night.
This couple's drinking daiquiri,
eyes entwined in daft delight.
Some touch teasingly

on the crowded floor or clutch tight
in intimate corners making fast embraces.
Orange on and off — yellow — red — white
mist puffs up, the music's pulse puts on pace.

Yet thou and I near-silver pair awaiting dawn,
not hot, now time's sands have run, but calm and warm.

HOMMAGE À HOLLANDE

Vous avez réussi
de justesse contre Nicolas Sarkozy.

Vous avez conduit, de Corrèze à la Rue de Solférino,
non pas une voiture de luxe, mais votre petite Clio.

Vous avez eu un contact avec la nuit lumineuse
quand l'avion a rencontré une tempête tumultueuse.

Vous avez dit, sans un mot, c'est toi qui bouges
en se heurtant à Mme Merkel sur le tapis rouge.

Vous aimez l'accordéon — les vieux vedettes.
Moi aussi j'adore le bal musette.

Les signes disent vous êtes modeste et original.
Pour ça, bonne continuation — vie politique et post-conjugale!

HOMAGE TO HOLLANDE
from the original French

You made it by a nose
versus Sarkozy.

You drove from Corrèze to the Rue de Solférino,
not in a posh car, but in your little *Clio*.

You made contact with lightning in the night
when your plane hit a violent storm in flight.

You said, without a word, it's you who must move
when, on the red carpet, you gave Mrs Merkel a shove.

You love the accordion and the old *vedettes*.
I adore them too and the *bal musette*.

Signs are you are modest, one of a kind,
so, carry on with life political — and post-marital, mind!

MAY DAY

You say you want to be strong at Brussels,
to flex your muscles.
You keep reiterating STRONG.
Economy strong
Security strong
Great Britain strong.
You want us to be the Continent's strongest,
that you'll fix it, albeit the Kingdom's exit.

In spring you went to the people
your strength indubitable.
You said, a vote cast for coalition — mayhem.
That's as may be, May Queen;
but if strong amounts to might
Is it right?
It might so easily go wrong.

Written two days before the general election of 8 June
2017, when the Conservative government, led by
Theresa May, lost its overall majority in Parliament.

UNSYSTEMATIC TRAVEL
TRAFFIC-LIGHT SYSTEM

We all know that Green means go,
that it connotes naivity and greenery
and that Red signals STOP,
in other words, don't go
unless for anger or hot blood
you'll board a plane for love.
But what about Amber if you want to do the samba
in Rio de Janeiro? Well, that's Red — enough said.
Surely, the light in the middle tells you to get ready,
put your foot on the pedal! Take off!
Now steady on! The Minister's recommended Amber *not* to travel
otherwise the 'road' to a healthy recovery will likely unravel.
Besides, doesn't yellow denote disease, something not nice
— Covid-19 to be precise.
It's clear that a traffic light system borders on the ridiculous
and that Amber's without a doubt ambiguous.

In April, 2021, the British government announced a so-called
'Traffic-Light System' which would allow international travel
to recommence during the Covid-19 pandemic.

E(XE)CU(TION)

They call you Head of State
Queen of the Low Lands
whose head adorns Dutch currency.
But there's a move afoot to loose it,
to lift it from your coinage.
Écu (or Euro) demands no sovereign
on its face, nor earmark on its back
but a headless change.

At Maastricht you condescended to give face:
'I will sacrifice my head,' you said,
'to Europa's body politic; thus dismembered
I'll still keep my crown to hand
in spite of such severance.'
In Wonderland, the Red Queen said to Alice
'Off with her head!'
but now it's the queen's turn to lose it.

POPPIES

The pinned poppy has a centre like a black hole; it sucks soldiers in.
The rest is red, redolent of blood, risk, cross, flame, passion,
men cut down, blown up, caught in Helmand's traps, snipers' sights,
boxed, brought back, and buried in Britannia's dark November.
The pinned poppy pricks a finger, startles the wearer into issues,
inquiry, the wherewithal of war, its spur and whereafters.
The reason's not in heroes — service, sacrifice, duty, country, God,
but in the pod: *Papaver* fields on Afghanistan's rich hills,
heroin harvest, cartel-trafficked, sinews of war, purchase of arms:
field piece, mortar, missile; munition, mine, timer,
war's panoply, forged from God's plant.

Monet painted them flaming away into a far field
a woman picking one in the drowsy afternoon.
In Flanders too they grew in soil touched by war
bodies bloodied, splayed in death
gas gasp, mask, last rasp, limbs lost, rotting,
rats, ditch run red, men retched in throe,
wounded to tents, agony — from poppy — opium-appeased,
relief, amputation, release or — after armistice —
day addiction, dread dreams: stained in stench,
trench, drenched — bullet, bursts, barbed wire,
discharge, detonation, flash, flesh, death . . .
'Nurse! Sister! Love! Wife! My medicine!'

A CROWNING

When main entrances are closed
and fathers go home to carve
pull out corks
dress up in red and white
talk baby talk;
when buildings
watched over by ageing men
are darkened
and registers covered
like birds at night in cages;
when clichés are carolled about,
and bloated parties heave
at crackers after gorging roast
with home tempers running high,
exhaustion sets in.
Brandy bottles, beer and gin
lie litter-empty,
stockings are left limp
parcels paper and string
cards shelved
all festive messages received.

Comes the second phase:
old guards go home
entrances are opened
lights levered on
goods marked down
cards marked up
and cash sucked
into shrill tills.
This is a time of coronation:
the beloved pound is crowned.

ON A CLOTHES LINE

One line is jeans,
casual as they come
into fashion in shapes sartorial;
high-rise, low and mid;
slim-fit, skinny crop and straight;
baggy, boot-cut, wide-cut, flared;
cigarette, boyfriend and pencil;
made of denim — derived *de Nîmes*,
named 'jeans' after Genoese *jeane*,
cloth stitched for seamen's trousers
in far-off sailing days.

Nowadays makers have large markets in mind.
They stray from indigo to other blues,
use dyes of green and grey,
tan and sand, khaki, olive, and maroon,
black, and even white.
They search for variation,
boldly turn out jeans bleached and faded.
When this fad's over slits, rips, shreds
and frays appear on thigh, knee, and shin,
'distressed' dress designed to grow
when drilled openings become the vogue.

One may wonder at future ventures into *prêt-à-porter*.
Jeans recycled from holed garment to whole?
or next in line — the emperor's new clothes?

CAMPERVAN-HAIKU CALENDAR

JANUARY
Snow lies on rooftops.
Powder crunches on the path.
The garage is shut.

FEBRUARY
A thaw has set in.
Gutters become rivulets.
I get out the van.

MARCH
In the cold of an
east wind, daffodils can bloom.
Engine still needs choke.

APRIL
Buds show on willows.
Showers batter the windscreen.
The roof starts to leak.

MAY
In weak warmth, cherry
blossom whitens the damp grass
and lightens the way.

JUNE
Late light evenings
make possible long road trips
and lengthy picnics.

JULY
Regatta excites
when camping in hot sunshine.
We see rowers race.

AUGUST
You sit on the shore,
swim in cooling North Sea waves;
sleep in cosy van.

SEPTEMBER
Sky's deep blue, pink-streaked
as I drive into the night
and late birds fly by.

OCTOBER
Days are shortening,
trees rust-coloured; roads glisten.
Headlights are switched on.

NOVEMBER
Wet leaves are falling.
Wipers go to-and-fro, to-
and-fro in the rain.

DECEMBER
I start the engine,
frost paints patterns on the glass.
I can't see a thing.

SMOKE

On seeing a cigarette advertisement
under which has been written,
'Have you seen the consequences?'

Between fingers ejecting a spiral of smoke
swirling skyward into a blue of oblivion
nails are yellowed like old paper,
lungs darkened like an old building.

Between lips, a glowing red of ash
pinpoints burning heat moving slowly
towards extinction and the sole of a foot.
Soon a match will flare like a firework

about to take flight, and a slow tapering
reignite the cycle of smooth sensation.
With smoke ingested through pulmonary pipes,
sooted walls of lungs decay, collapse

into disorder, decline and fell disease.
Constant coughing shakes the frame;
expansion of ribs, contraction of diaphragm
falter into final fall.

ASTHMATIC

You breathe in too much
out too little,
your lungs, two full balloons,
feel about to burst into emphysema,
expiration even.
The in-and-out of your breath
finds no balance in respiration.

No high pillow will give relief
nor tablets under the tongue.
You'll stay sleepless
in the sanatorium,
stare out at the empty night
until first call, first light
and the day's inspiration.

PROSTATE PROCESS

I. CHECK UP

No, I don't smoke.
Drink? I'm a sensible bloke.
Just an occasional tot,
need to — you know what — a lot, a lot.
Yes, walks aplenty
every morning in the park
up with the proverbial lark,
keeps me slim and healthy.
Blood test? Yes, please do.
Can you find the vein?
No, Nurse, no pain.
Thanks. Time to go.

2. APPOINTMENT

Your PSA is rather high.
We need to know why?
Lie down and I'll have a feel.
Relax! It's no big deal.
Does it hurt when I push?
That's good, no great rush.
I'll put you in for a hospital date,
better catch it early rather than late.

3. CONSULTANT

How many times at night?
Do you feel the flow is tight?
What is your health situation?
Are you taking medication?
Are you keeping well in yourself?
Have you had previous problems of health?
I'll fill you in for a diagnosis.
It may, or may not, confirm my prognosis.

4. BIOPSY

He clips away at my anesthetized behind.
I, lying on my side, face the nurse
Sam — Samantha.
He clips away — clip, clip —
she holds me in conversation
as he clips — keeps me talking.
I tell her I'm a poet — odd thing
when inspected from behind
with Samantha and I chatting
and he clip-clipping.

5. CONSULTANT

Long wait at Outpatients . . .
patience . . . patience . . . patience . . .
My name is called.
Sit here. Mr C. will see you soon.
Ushered into a small room,
voices from behind a door
wait some more . . . more . . . more.
Mr C. and Nurse Lucy enter with the news.
You're listed number 8 — not too late
for treatment. I'll put you in for a scan
as soon as we possibly can.

6. BONE SCAN

My head's in a moving cylinder.
It follows the length of my prostrate body
with a whiiiiirrring . . .
I lie dead still as told,
think of living extra-terrestrially,
robotic, free of gravity
where there's no ill weight.

7. MEDICATION

No Cancer in the bones!
Prescription: hormones
for a quarter,
tablet to be taken with water
at set time each day
with precision — come what may!
After which, if PSA's low
and urine's not too slow
we'll start with radiotherapy.

THREE MONTHS LATER

8. FLOW TEST

My belly's bursting!
I've filled up to the top of my tank —
Can't stop, must evacuate.
Nurse doesn't mind, she's kind,
patient, she'll wait till I'm ready.
It's not long 'til the flow feels strong
and I'm in for the test.
At best I've peed a bit
after which Nurse loosens my belt
puts something soggy on my tummy,
takes a reading for a fine result.

94

9. PHONE CALL

Lucy calling!
Your PSA is down to point 2.
Good!
Your flow test's through.
It's as it should.
Keep taking the pills for your ills,
therapy will start in June.
Not soon?
No, three months more to wait,
Mr C. says you'll be ready for it at this rate.
We'll write to tell you the start-up date.

THREE MONTHS LATER

10. LETTER

Dear B. Thank you for reviewing this gentleman's notes.
He certainly has an obstructive flow rate.
His imaging shows a large intravesical prostate.
This will need to be resected
before radiotherapy can be started.
Yours sincerely, C.

11. OPERATION

Wheeled into the anaesthetist's cubicle
I see her young, ready with a needle.
'Sorry, Sir, it didn't work this time.
I'll try again.' I see she's nervous — a novice.
I say, don't worry, and fall into sublime . . .

12. POST OP

When I come round, I can't stop talking.
The man standing by my trolley listens
as though used to patients blathering.
He pushes me towards my ward and hastens
off to the next unconscious rising to the surface.

It's a three-day stay tended by Jane,
cared for by Carmen on loan from Spain,
looked after by African East End Amy
and others from the international nursing fraternity;
fed bland English meals by a local lady,
from the end of the bed, seen by doctors daily,
till catheter removed by Sister Maylie
and I can leave the ward for home — but frailly.

13. MEDICAL DISCHARGE SUMMARY
Large median lobe, poor flow, resected
and small amount of lat lobe.
Three ways catheter inserted.
First day post op was stable,
irrigation stopped.
Radiotherapy now enabled.

THREE MONTHS LATER

14. PLANNING 1
There will be twenty afternoon sessions.
To identify the precise area to be treated
a computer tomography scanner will be used
to take a digital portrait for your treatment records.
You will need to come with a full bladder
and empty bowel. Here's a medicine to ensure the latter.
And here's a form for your consent.
Resigned, I pick up the paper — and sign.

15. PLANNING 2
My shoes are off and my trousers down.
I'm under the scanner: start of the plan.
I'm left for a while with the lights set low
until two nurses return with their rods.
They pinpoint the place the waves will touch
and mark my belly with a permanent period.
When the measuring's done and I'm on my feet
I pull up my trousers and put on my shoes,
then wait for the CT scan to be checked
and the diligent surveyors to be thanked.

16. SESSIONS 1–20
We come in December cold, my wife and I,
sit and wait with time passing by.
We're not bored, nor feel ignored
for there's a TV with antiques under the hammer,
tea to make with milk and sugar
and cold water to fill the bladder.
My carer-consort has her tablet to absorb her,
I've got my scattered thoughts to order.
We're running late, but it's no matter,
we might even be inclined to chatter — even better to natter.
Then a nurse calls out my name and I'm lying down again.

This is the treatment room. I lie on the treatment couch.
Two therapy radiographers set about aligning me.
The hospital leaflet tells me to lie still,
but that I'm allowed to breathe normally —
Do I detect a modicum of horizontal hospital humour?
(I'm backing up this wit with blended assonance and consonance
and a little alliteration.)
Once adjusted, the machine's set in equipoise
over my pinpointed belly. I'm left alone in low light
and noise, am seen on screen and heard on intercom
should I shout out with unease.
In twenty relaxed minutes, the radiographers return
and I'm on my feet again, my trousers up and shoes on,
ready to rejoin my waiting wife
for a walk back home in the evening cold,
this repeated twenty weekday times one weary winter
when our star was out.

SIX MONTHS LATER

17. CONSULTANT TO GP
[. . .] this pleasant gentleman,
accompanied by his partner [. . .]
is absolutely well in himself.
His PSA [originally 7.4] was reported as 0.3.
At this point I plan to see him back in six months
with prior PSA. Kind regards.

18. ODE TO THE KNIGHTS OF THE NHS
Here is a final poem of praise
to counter the media's maze
of censure unleashed against our knights,
our leading lights, who seek to put to rights
the plight of those in illness or in pain
with no thought of egotistical self-serving gain.
They who spend long hours dedicated to the sick
through thick and thin, and the din of daft diatribe
and unholy media muck. To you I say, congrats,
to them, get lost you rats!
I'll make no bones about it, and confess
my love for the knights of the NHS.

SAILING AWAY
for my brother, on his remission from cancer

Hear this celebratory poem
addressed to all who know him.
Tim, stout-hearted to the last
has nailed his colours to the mast
of recovery, like an Olympic sailor set on gold,
with tacks and gybes both passionate and bold,
he's crossed the line to calm water
and now stands firm on the quarter.
So here's to Tim for ample years
to come. We wish him friendly fair winds. Cheers!

ODE TO OPAL

in memory of Opal Markin-Reeves

You asked me to celebrate your name.
O, yes, I'll write it in large character
Opining all my praise
Pressing print into impression
A first edition to be highly sought
Letters coerced to spell a name.
I'll mark in script as reeves once did
Authoritative bailiff's book.
I'll play steward to your passing[1] worth
With words no ledger ever mistook.

When Anna crawled on cottage floor
And I, lone father, acted constant guardian
Sunk in a mother's madness
You stepped in to delight her
With pied beauty, brilliant
In the north room where she played.
Yours was a precious presence
With fine play of colour
As marked as print on plate glass
Remarkable as stone of fire, *upala*, gem.

---

[1] unsurpassed

ELEGY FOR A BELL-RINGER

in memory of Denis Thompson

In ancient times a poet called upon the Muse
To sum up worthy weeds to clothe his mourning.
He'd conjure up a rural scene and make himself a shepherd
And in procession ask the mourners their place when death had come.
He'd set forth in flow of words the flower-smothered bier
And order nature's sufferance as though wounded by such loss.
He'd reflect on the dues of Providence and the scourge of current sin
And in high-flown fashion resort to blown-up pastoralism.

What need I to indulge in such embellishment
To mourn your unjust passing, friend?
— Unless to pull 'bell' out of it.
Only picture you with your gracious Mischa,
Geared, intrepid, walking on wind-swept moor
Or in town trim catch you lift a glass to all with in-born cheer;
See you sports-shirted on big bike grip strong bars
Or stand to be snapped at St Paul's among cared-for flowers;
But most, in Devon tower, pull in a powerful peal of eight,
With you, Denis, on the biggest bell there to calibrate
The changes; and, too, in close garage host ringers on home bells,
To know you leave a swell of cheer for friends to call you by
And above all, peals of love for your mourning Mischa to adore
As with rope in hand she rues her missing dodge in the three/four.

FABLE

When deciduous trees
turn to golden brown
and a chill wind warns
of Arctic snow
the geese fly south
to warmer climes
in V formation
their wings

breeze
in a fair and friendly
their sails drawing well
of the rearward birds
easing the flight
lift up the air
full canvas

When the goose
at the apex tires
she drops back in rotation
to give another bird
the lead —

the pacemaker
honk-honking
cry encouragement
and those in the rear

When a goose
falls out of formation
the air drags
at the lone bird
until

to the very letter
and flies
it rejoins the flock
knowing better

and when one is shot
or falls ill
two geese descend
with the ailing bird
staying by him
till

rest in formation
and rejoining
they catch up with the flock
then launching out again
he flies — or dies —

MOTH

after D. H. Lawrence

A moth came to my bathroom on a cold Friday.

In the deep white of the tub it lay back-stretched,
struggling.

I could have slid open the window for it to take flight,
but seeing the insect lie death-fluttering
in its metal tomb, I left the window latched.

I came to my bathroom on cold Sunday.

In the deep white of the tub
lay black specks, the moth's body gone.

Came to mind the two Marys at the grave after Golgotha,
struck by bolt of light, moved by quake,
they seeing the stone rolled back.

GIFT

for Thérèse

This present's for you my jewel,
diamond strong, clear as star,
permanent in the firmament.

This present's for you my star,
celestial-steady, dear as diamond
on prince's ringed fingers.

This present's for you my Love,
my sparkler, bright as night when
kings came with golden gifts.

LOOKING WEST

I WANDERED along the vine row, grapes near to ripening in the southern sun. In a few weeks, the migrant workers would be arriving to take in the harvest — women with wily fingers who snip at speed along each row, and broad-shouldered muscly men, heavers of filled barrels onto waiting lorries.

At the end of a row, I saw a figure silhouetted in the lowering sun.

'Hello!' I called out and approached him, wondering who it might be. He was bearded with long hair to his shoulders and was perhaps thirty. He seemed out of place among the vines. I could have imagined him playing an electric guitar at a concert in a football stadium, or rolling grass in a relaxed way at a Dutch camp site.

'Can I help you?' I asked.

'Tell me . . . .' He paused looking around. 'Which vineyard is this?'

'Pierre's Place,' I replied.

'That's fine — I've been looking for it.'

'Oh —'

'I'm here to take in the harvest.'

'But we haven't started picking. It's too early. Have you come from far?'

'From the north and east and west, and from the south.'

He saw my puzzled look — and smiled. To fill an awkward silence I asked him:

'Would you like a drink?'

'Thank you — yes — it's been a hot day, although now this part of the earth's turning itself away from the sun.'

I was struck by his odd way of referring to the sunset.

'We'll go to the house then,' I said, and started walking to the end of the row. When I turned round to see if he was following, I caught his head lit up in the semi-round of the sun. It was like the figure in the stained glass window in the apse of our village church, only this was a living halo which told me what harvest it was he had come to gather in.